T0077957

No-Nonsense Practical Wisdom 101

Life Quotes to instruct, guide, empower.

Janice Johns Redman

Illustrations by Madeline B. Shearer

AuthorHouse™
1663 Liberty Drive
Bloomington, IN 47403
www.authorhouse.com
Phone: 833-262-8899

Published by AuthorHouse 06/25/2022

ISBN: 978-1-6655-5985-0 (sc)
ISBN: 978-1-6655-5983-6 (hc)
ISBN: 978-1-6655-5984-3 (e)

Library of Congress Control Number: 2022909218

Print information available on the last page.

authorHOUSE®

No-Nonsense Practical Wisdom 101

Life Quotes to instruct, guide, empower.

For Victoria Lynn Long-Coleman, Ph.D.

As soap is to the body, so is laughter to the soul.

Jewish Proverb

Contents

Life Quotes to instruct, guide, empower.

Ability

Ability

Accountability is your ability to give an account for your actions. Responsibility is your ability to be responsible for what's required of you.

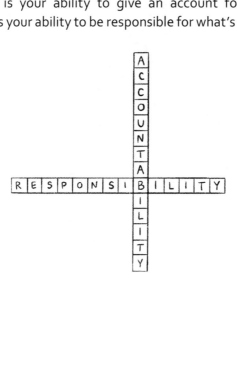

Age

Age

Age is just a number and it depends on how much emphasis you place on that number.

16 95 64
43 30 51 18 10
25 6 12 101 76
88 4 9 27
21 32

Anger

Anger

Anger is only one letter short of danger.

Eleanor Roosevelt

Apology

Apology

The best apology is to exclude what the other person did. Don't mix apology with blame.

Apprehensions

Apprehensions

When you spend time worrying, you're simply using your imagination to create anxiety, fear, doubt, uncertainty, suspicion and more unnecessary apprehensions.

Ask

Ask

Don't be afraid to ask, search for answers, and when opportunity knocks open its door and walk through with boldness.

> *Ask and it will be given to you;*
> *Seek and you will find;*
> *Knock and the door will be opened to you.*

Matthew 7:7 (NIV)

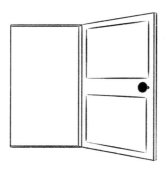

Better

Better

You may look back and wish choices made were different, but at times decisions were based on ignorance, inexperience and without guidance. Nevertheless, reflect on this:

I can only achieve my best as I become better at what I do.

Chances

Chances

If you're not sure where you're going, chances are you'll end up somewhere else.

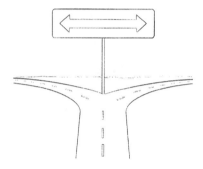

Change

Change

Change can be beautiful when we are brave enough to evolve with it, and change can be brutal when we fearfully resist.

Bryant H. McGill

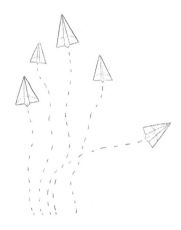

Character

Character

Your actions become habits, your habits develop character, and your character reveals integrity or lack of it.

reputation
personality
Uprightness

Choices

Choices

You become the choices you've made, even when you made the decision not to make a choice.

Command

Command

When chaos invades your space, command order, peace and stability in your mind, body and life affairs.

Serenity

Compelled

Compelled

We are more compelled to remain as we are than compelled to change.

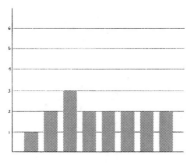

~

Continue

~

Continue

At first you start, next continue.

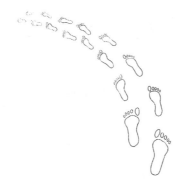

Decision

Decision

A mistake repeated more than once is a decision.

Paulo Coelho

$$5+5=11 \quad 1+1=3$$
$$3+3=7 \quad 4+4=9$$
$$7+7=15 \quad 2+2=5$$
$$6+6=13 \quad 9+9=19$$
$$10+10=21 \quad 8+8=17$$

Decline

Decline

If it's difficult to refuse commitments, gracefully decline with these responses:

- I appreciate your offer, but...
- It's kind of you to consider me, however...
- I'm not be able to commit this time; thank you for understanding...

Commitments should be a welcomed responsibility, not demanding obligations.

No, thank you.

Denial

Denial

Denial prevents one from facing reality, confronting challenges, and working through difficulties.

Effort

Effort

It takes no effort to be kind, but it takes effort to be unkind.

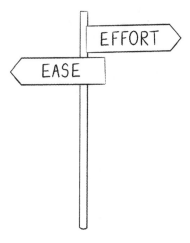

Ego

Ego

Self-ego seeks validation to win arguments with:

- *I'm right, you're wrong*
- *We agree to disagree*
- *Get over it*

What's the point for ego to win? Just call it a truce.

Engaged

Engaged

Be an engaged listener just as you desire the same consideration when you speak.

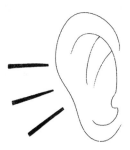

Exchange

Exchange

Caring prevents neglect,

Kindness supersedes meanness,

Politeness replaces rudeness,

Love banishes hate.

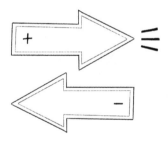

~

Experience

~

Experience

No one has the right to disrupt my journey that ultimately keeps me from experiences, discoveries, and lessons I must learn.

Extraordinary

Extraordinary

Our most extraordinary moments of achievement are times we whole-heartily expressed love toward others.

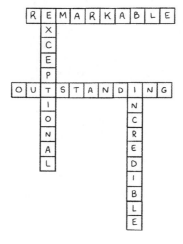

Failure

Failure

Failure is not a disaster, but to remain a failure becomes your disaster.

Fear

Fear

Don't allow fear to make life-time decisions for you.

Forgiveness

Forgiveness

Asking for forgiveness is like planting seeds. Knowing it takes time for seeds to germinate, sprout roots and grow, accepting forgiveness also takes time.

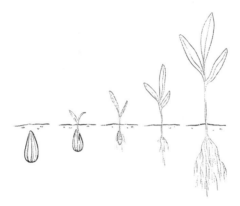

Friendship

Friendship

The only way to have a friend is to be one.

Ralph Waldo Emerson

Generous

Generous

Selflessness encourages generosity.

Growth

Growth

Growth is optional.

John Maxwell

Help!

Help!

Hello Eternal Loving Presence!

Michael Bernard Beckwith

Higher

Higher

Who gives you constructive criticism, practical advice, and challenges you to elevate higher within your circle of friends?

Humility

Humility

Ego seeks to correct and be right, but humility endeavors to listen and understand.

Hunger

Hunger

You can want something or you can hunger for it. The difference between the two is wishful, would-be notions, or pursuing that thing with purpose, intention, sacrifice.

Idleness

Idleness

Having nothing to do and lots of time to do nothing defines idleness.

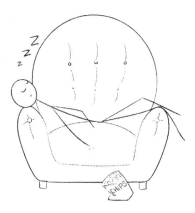

Incompatible

Incompatible

If your life demonstrates solid ground, you cannot align with one whose life is sinking sand.

Judging

Judging

Judging a person does not define who they are. It defines who you are.

Wayne Dyer

Laughter

Laughter

The sound of laughter is so contagious it requires no medical remedy.

Lesson

Lesson

There's a lesson to learn from flowers. Be it Petunias, Irises, Geraniums, or Daffodils, whether in flower beds, gardens or assorted pots, they never compete with each other.

Letting Go

Letting Go

The way trees know when to let go of their leaves is how we should let go of relationships, places, and things as their seasons end.

Liberation

Liberation

Forgiving yourself liberates you from being stuck in the past.

Listen

Listen

There are times when listening with your heart replaces listening with your ears.

Living

Living

People live to be angry.

People live to be critical.

People live to be drama.

People live to be jealous.

People live to be offended.

How do you live?

Live life to the fullest

Love

Love

Love is not manipulative.

Love does not pointlessly correct others.

Love does not always seek to have the last word.

love

~

My Temple

~

My Temple

What's in my temple that needs cleaning out?

What's dwelling in my heart that should be settled, released, disposed?

What from my past hangs on walls, displays on shelves, kept in closets?

What rooms are safekeepers for unforgiveness?

Where are unresolved emotions stockpiled?

What's in my temple no longer beneficial, valuable, purposeful?

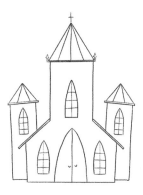

Never Forget

Never Forget

Whether thoughtful deeds, compliments, or unkind words, people never forget how you made them feel.

Next Steps

Next Steps

Prayer is not a crutch for procrastination. Understand that prayers also open pathways for *to do's, next steps, action plans.*

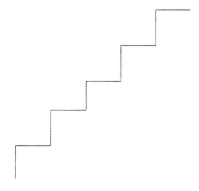

Only

Only

As the slogan goes, you only live once. Actually, we live every day but only die once.

Opportunity

Opportunity

Old ways won't open new doors.

Author unknown

Other Side

Other Side

What's on the other side of your fear?

Patience

Patience

Knowing where you are going far exceeds how fast you can get there. Impatience gets you nowhere.

Peace

Peace

Peace is precious so savor moments of quiet, stillness, serenity.

Perception

Perception

When you disagree, the other point of view can be just as persuasive as yours. It's all about perception which can appear right, wrong, or indifferent.

Possibilities

Possibilities

Faith takes us to places of unknown possibilities.

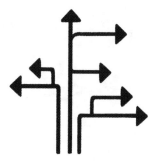

Presence

Presence

The right words to say when someone experiences loss may not come to mind; however, the power of your presence speaks volumes.

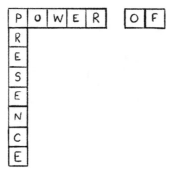

Quiet Times

Quiet Times

Your quiet time allows for mental relaxation and clarity.

Release

Release

Forgiveness releases hurt, pain, anger, resentment— emotions that cause greater harm.

Rest

Rest

It's okay to take some "me time"—give yourself permission to rest.

Rest
Relax
Repeat

Revelation

Revelation

Marriages don't cause problems, they reveal them.

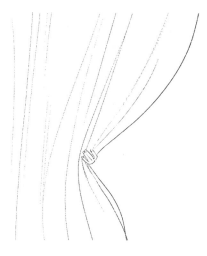

Seasons

Seasons

Just as you journey throughout seasons of your life, respect where others are on their journey.

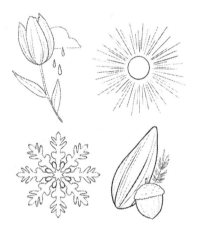

~

Self-Assurance

~

Self-Assurance

To be sure and confident, to be in the right place, to elevate to higher heights is believing, belonging, becoming.

Becoming

Self-Respect

Self-Respect

If you don't love, respect or value yourself, why expect others to treat you any different?

Give Respect
Get Respect

Shine

Shine

The Sun does not ask *How am I doing? Do you feel the warmth? Do you see sunlight?* It just shines.

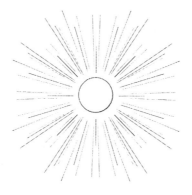

Silence

Silence

Unlike the mouth, ears don't get us in trouble. You cannot argue, debate, or disagree with silence.

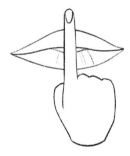

Stillness

Stillness

Your season of stillness becomes an opportunity to renew, redo, reset, realign, redirect, readjust, recharge, release.

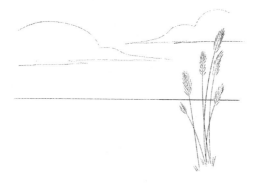

Strength

Strength

To be anti-fragile is to be courageous, determined, resilient.

Take Time

Take Time

Taking time to enjoy life is like taking time to enjoy your favorite ice cream cone.

Today

Today

Today becomes tomorrow that had been yesterday,

Yesterday was the today that became tomorrow,

Tomorrow was the yesterday that had been today.

Truth

Truth

The truth can hurt, or you can feel good about it.

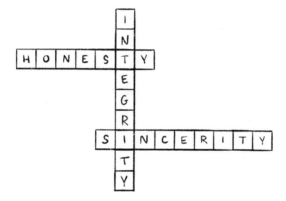

Unfolding

Unfolding

Just as blossoming flowers unfold their array of beauty, so is the way love unfolds.

Valuable

Valuable

A diamond, pearl, or gold tossed into mud do not lose their value. Likewise, whatever you've been through or when at your lowest point, you're still valuable.

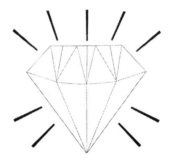

Viewpoint

Viewpoint

The man who views the world at 50 the same as he did at 20 has wasted 30 years of his life.

Muhammad Ali

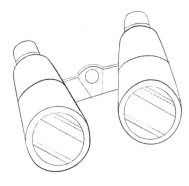

What Matters Most

What Matters Most

Care more about your integrity than your success.

Ethical

Honesty

Values

Truthfulness

Words

Words

The tongue can speak harmful, damaging words, and so does the thumb when texting and tweeting. So, which is it—your tongue or your thumb?

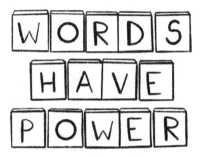

Work Week Gratitude

Work Week Gratitude

Marvelous Monday

Terrific Tuesday

Wonderful Wednesday

Thankful Thursday

Fabulous Friday

Worries

Worries

Worry has babies that creates more worries to worry about. Understand this when consumed with worries:

- 92% of things we worry about do not occur
- 2% of things we worry about do occur, but are easily resolved
- 6% of things we worry about do occur, but there's nothing we can do about it

Author of Data Unknown

Years

Years

In our younger years we look like our parents, in our older years we look like our choices.

Yes and No

Yes and No

A hundred *No's* are less painful than one insincere *Yes*.

Ancient Chinese Proverb

You

You

Take into account that it's not always about you.

$$\begin{array}{r} \text{you} \\ + \ \text{you} \\ \hline \text{You?} \end{array}$$

Your Way

Your Way

Life is too short convincing others that things should be a certain way—
your way.

Also by Janice Johns Redman

Uncovered Treasures
From My Heart to Yours

Printed in the United States
by Baker & Taylor Publisher Services